Quest to Heal

A Guide to Healing Your History of Loss, Grief, Abuse, or Trauma

Quest to Heal

A Guide to Healing Your History of Loss, Grief, Abuse, or Trauma

Marsha Ferrick Heiden, PhD., BCC

Author

Quest to Heal

A Guide to Healing Your History of Loss, Grief, Abuse, or Trauma

Written by Marsha Ferrick Heiden, PhD., BCC

Illustrated by Marie Billings Dalton

Marsha Ferrick Heiden, PhD, BCC

Amara Quest, Inc.

8322 State Route 305

Garrettsville, OH 44231

http://www.amaraquest.com

To my clients who survived, and now thrive!

This is my Quest

Date

Table of Contents

Preparation for Your Quest 1

    Symptom Management 1

        Re-Experiencing 1

        Avoidance 3

        Negative Cognitions and Mood 4

        Arousal 5

    Support 6

Environmental Safety 7

    Safe Work Space 9

    Safety Strategy 14

Your Knapsack 17

    Measuring Distress 17

    Gaining Dual Awareness 18

    Utilizing Awareness to Manage Emotions 22

        Awareness is the First Step in Changing Behavior 22

        Importance of Insight 24

        Lack of Insight 25

The Quest Begins 27

    Trauma/Grief Time-Line 27

    The Challenge 31

Claiming the Holy Grail 33

    Telling the Story of Your Quest 36

"Two roads diverged in a yellow wood, . . .

In leaves no step had trodden back...

Yet knowing how way leads on to way, I doubted if I should ever come back.

I shall be telling this with a sigh Somewhere ages and ages hence:

Two roads diverged in a wood, and I— I took the one less traveled by,

And that has made all the difference."

The Road Not Taken
By Robert Frost

Preparation for Your Quest

The Quest to Heal is a powerful transformational journey, but it is not an easy one. If you are even thinking about traveling this road to healing, you have a great deal of courage. Remember courage is not lack of fear, but acknowledging your fear and doing it anyway. Healing from loss, grief, abuse, or trauma is not an easy journey so preparation is paramount.

Symptom Management

The first step in symptom management is to identify the PTSD Symptoms that are interfering and impacting your life. Keep in mind you may not be experiencing all these symptoms, and some symptoms you may be already effectively managing. Remember when you are on a journey things do change and as some symptoms lessen others may emerge, and the challenge will be to learn to manage these symptoms as they occur. Symptoms occur in four major areas re-experiencing, avoidance, negative thoughts and mood, and arousal.

Re-Experiencing

Re-experiencing covers spontaneous memories of the traumatic event, recurrent dreams related to it, flashbacks or other intense or prolonged psychological distress.

- ❖ Dissociating
- ❖ Flashbacks
- ❖ Nightmares
- ❖ Physiological distress to known or unknown triggers

- ❖ Anxiety
- ❖ Body symptoms, often not medically explainable
- ❖ Intrusive thoughts, unwanted thoughts that reoccur

Do you exhibit any of these symptoms? If so, which ones, how, and when do they appear? Are they getting in the way of your day to day functioning?

Avoidance

Avoidance of distressing memories, thoughts, feelings or external reminders of the event.

- ❖ Addictions or addictive behaviors
- ❖ Isolating

Do you exhibit any of these symptoms? If so, which ones, how, and when do they appear? Are they getting in the way of your day to day functioning?

Negative Cognitions and Mood

Negative cognitions and mood represents a myriad of feelings, from a persistent and distorted sense of blame of self or others, to estrangement from others or markedly diminished interest in activities, to an inability to remember key aspects of the event.

❖ Blank spots in your memory
❖ Apathy, not caring about things
❖ Feeling detached from others
❖ Few emotions, numbness
❖ No sense of a future
❖ Sensitive, intense emotional arousal

Do you exhibit any of these symptoms? If so, which ones, how, and when do they appear? Are they getting in the way of your day to day functioning?

Arousal

Arousal is marked by aggressive, reckless or self-destructive behavior, sleep disturbances, hypervigilance or related problems.

- ❖ Sleeping difficulties
- ❖ Irritable, and angry
- ❖ Trouble concentrating
- ❖ Easily startled
- ❖ Difficulty with adult functioning, relationship may be problematic
- ❖ Self-harm

How will you manage your symptoms during your Quest? Be specific. What skills will you use for each symptom?

If you are having difficulty managing any of the above symptoms I recommend *The PTSD Workbook: Simple, Effective Techniques for Overcoming Traumatic Stress Symptoms* (M.B. Williams & S. Poijula), or the *PTSD Coach Online* on the ptsd.va.gov website. It is possible that symptom management may be enough for some people, but for others managing symptoms will not be enough to pursue a fulfilling and joy filled life. Make sure that you can manage your symptoms effectively, be able to be and keep yourself safe before progressing.

Support

"It doesn't interest me what you do for a living. I want to know ... if you have touched the centre of your own sorrow, if you have been opened by life's betrayals or have become shriveled and closed from fear of further pain. I want to know if you can sit with pain, mine or your own, without moving to hide it, or fade it, or fix it... It doesn't interest me if the story you are telling me is true. I want to know if you can disappoint another to be true to yourself... I want to know if you can see Beauty even when it is not pretty every day. And if you can source your own life from its presence. I want to know if you can live with failure, yours and mine, and still stand at the edge of the lake and shout to the silver of the full moon, 'Yes.' It doesn't interest me to know where you live or how much money you have. I want to know if you can get up after the night of grief and despair, weary and bruised to the bone and do what needs to be done to feed the children. It doesn't interest me who you know or how you came to be here. I want to know if you will stand in the centre of the fire with me and not shrink back ... I want to know what sustains you from the inside when all else falls away. I want to know if you can be alone with yourself and if you truly like the company you keep in the empty moments."

Oriah Mountain Dreamer

Ultimately you will do this work alone, however having support is imperative for this journey. Support may be a partner, friend, or therapist that can be a nonjudgmental listener and hold a space for you to share your thoughts and feelings. Find someone that does not want to fix you, but can allow you to move through your process at your own rate, or speed while maintaining patience and empathetic detachment. I recommend working with a psychologist that is trained in CBT imaginal prolonged exposure therapy. Who will be your primary support while you are on this quest?

Environmental Safety

Are you safe from harm or abuse from yourself or anyone else? If you are not safe, do not go beyond this first chapter. You cannot heal while in the midst of a battlefield. Is your physical environment safe? Why or why not?

If your physical environment is not safe what can you do to change it? Remember do not proceed with this work until you are living in a safe environment.

Safe Work Space

If you have an environment that is safe find a place to work within that environment that is particularly comfortable and private. Describe this place and why it will be a great place to be while on your journey towards healing.

What will you do to help the space to feel protected?

What time of day will you work? Set aside at least two hours for your work each day. You may not need all of it, but it is best to plan for too much time then too little.

The space must be kept private from others. How will you manage that?

What will you have with you that will make your space feel safer? You might consider a talisman or amulet used as an object for protection or comfort.

What will you have with you in your space to help you manage your symptoms? For example, a comfortable pillow, a good luck charm, or peaceful, soothing pictures.

Safety Strategy

Create a safety plan for yourself to follow if you begin to feel as if you are unable to keep yourself safe.

What skills will you try? Keep a written list available. List at least three. Consider soothing music, focusing on your breathing, word or number games.

Who will you call? Are there phone numbers in your phone? Are they easily accessible?

Where will you go? Places that are safe in your living space or outside your home (if you are able to drive).

Create a collage or drawing of your safe space. Remember the space is private for your use only. Use pictures, words, drawings or objects to help you create a safe space in your mind as well as creating a safe physical location.

What objects can you carry with you that will remind you of your safe space while you are out in the world?

Your Knapsack

On your quest you will need tools as well as skills to mark your progress. You will need to understand these tools and have these skills in order to proceed on your journey.

Measuring Distress

SUDs stands for Subjective Unit of Distress. Throughout this next section SUDs will be useful for you in identifying your level of distress. SUDs describe the emotions you are feeling in the moment with zero being a level of no intensity and 100 being very intense. So, first let's identify your comfort zone, warning zone, and danger zone.

Zones. On the next page in the left hand column beside each SUD level number write down for each number if that level is in your comfort zone. Many people are comfortable with low levels of distress. So they would write the word "Comfort" beside the number 0, 10, 20, and 30. People will sometimes notice a place where their Distress Levels are climbing yet they are still managing the distress with some effort at these numbers. For this level write in "Warning." Warning levels vary a great deal depending on your ability to tolerate distress, and your self- awareness. However, some people feel like they go from 0 to 100 rapidly and often have little or no warning zone. "Warning" zones typically range in the 30 to 80's range. "Danger" zones are the levels of distress in which individuals tend to become flooded with emotion whether it is sadness, or anger, or stonewalling (shutting down). The "Danger" zone for an individual can begin at any number, but for most people the "Danger" zone is in the 80, 90, and 100's. The important part is to reflect your own zones accurately for yourself.

Anchor Points. Anchor points identify three points of reference for you to determine your SUDs levels consistently across times and events. Your anchor point for 0 is a time or event when you feel or have felt no distress. Your anchor point for 100 is a time or event when you have felt the most distress you have ever felt. Your anchor point for 50 is a time or event that is a mid-distress point between 0 and 100. When you are asked for a SUDs you compare it to your three anchor points to give you a sense of the number you will give to your current distress.

Distress Levels		
Zone	**SUD**	**Anchor Points***
	100	*
	90	
	80	
	70	
	60	
	50	*
	40	
	30	
	20	
	10	
	0	*

Gaining Dual Awareness

It is important to realize that current sensations (feelings) may trigger old feelings (sensations) from the past. This becomes confusing for trauma survivors and those around them because it is difficult to sort out what is about the past and what is about the present. Reactions are often huge in the present and feel justified to the trauma survivor, but to others the trauma survivor may appear over reactive, over sensitive or crazy. Therefore, it is important to understand that whenever we are having a big feeling it is not just about the present, but also and probably foremost, about the past.

Whenever you are overcome by any overwhelming feeling try to notice and name it. Tell yourself, "Wow, this is interesting. I am really reacting to... (whatever or whoever is in the current environment)." Try not to react in the moment, but just observe. When you are able to get away from the current situation (at least in the beginning) look at your feelings and what you believed triggered them. Ask

18

yourself where, when or with whom have you felt this way? See if you can get clear about the past before you deal with the issue in the present. Have someone that you trust help you to sort it out. Often you will find that the present is not the problem, but another opportunity to gain increased awareness. As you gain more awareness you will have the ability to modify your behaviors in the present to be more effective and to process those very intense historical feelings so they begin to dissipate and occur only rarely. This will take time and practice so be patient with yourself.

Consider a mildly distressing event. Close your eyes and go back to the event. Note your physiological reaction to remembering the event. Do you feel increased anxiety or distress? What do you notice? Temperature? Breathing? Thoughts?

Now come back to the room. Note the details of the room, windows, wall color, window treatments, furniture, floor, rugs, paintings, pictures, décor, sounds, smells, and scent. Again note your physiological reaction to being in the present moment. Do you feel less anxiety or distress? What do you notice? Temperature? Breathing? Thoughts? How have they changed from exercise one?

Now can you do exercise one and two at the same time? Write down what happens as you try to do this exercise. What do you notice? End this exercise with being fully present to your current environment.

Utilizing Awareness to Manage Emotions

Specific Combination of Physical Sensations = A Specific Emotional Label

You may have learned early in life to assign a specific emotional label to a combination of physical sensations you experienced in your body. However, if you did learn these early life lessons about emotions abuse, trauma, loss, and grief may have impacted your ability to identify and express those feelings in an effective way. Therefore, you may have turned to behaviors that number your internal sensations to avoid dealing with your feelings because it was not safe to do so.

Awareness is the First Step in Changing Behavior

Have you ever had one of those moments of reflection in which you thought why on earth did I say or do that? Share an example.

If you have you are certainly not alone. Most of us have had countless occasions over the years to ponder our thoughtless choice of word or deed. Typically, as you get older and your self-awareness increases those moments diminish in frequency. Why does this occur? In simple terms when you lack awareness you react in your environment controlled by your most basic emotions typically fear (Diagram 2 below). When you are young you do not necessarily reflect on why you did what you did, you figure out what is effective in the environment and repeat it. However, as your environment changes you find yourself repeating these behaviors with less than effective outcomes. You then become frustrated at your lack of ability to adapt in ways that will aid you in getting your needs met in the current environment. Often you fail to realize that it is your lack of adaption that is problematic and blame it on others or the environment. Until one day you start to realize that it keeps happening over and over again to you and not others in your environment.

When you first gain awareness (Diagram 1 below) you start to recognize what you are doing or saying that is not working for you. However, it may be difficult to figure out what to do next. Awareness comes in many forms and can be experienced at several levels. You can be aware of (observe) your body sensations, beliefs, thoughts and perceptions and urges to act. You can then describe to yourself what is going on. Take note of these facts. Then you suspend the action into the environment and with your new awareness you now have a choice about how you chose to act. Often times you need to discover new ways of being and acting in your environment that are effective. Often this means learning new skills to utilize, and make a conscientious effort to change. As you begin to act with awareness in your environment you notice the impact you are having on others and the environment, this is called reflection.

Reflection allows you to determine effective behaviors in your environment, and adapt in ways that will aid you in getting your needs met. If an action or reaction was ineffective, you need to plan a more effective strategy for the next time. The more you are aware and the more you are able to reflect, the more you will be able to determine how effective you are in all areas of your life, and where you need to continue to develop a broader range of skills.

Consider a time that you reflected on something that you had said or done. What did you discover? How did that change your behavior as you moved on?

Importance of Insight

Effective Choice with Awareness and Reflection. With awareness you <u>act</u> in your environment controlled by your wise mind. Your wise mind is that inner part of you that knows that something is true for you. It is quiet, peaceful, and is a valid answer or best choice for you. Awareness comes in many forms and can be experienced at several levels. You can be aware of (observe) your body sensations, beliefs, thoughts and perceptions and urges to act. You can then describe to yourself what is going on. Take note of these facts. Then you suspend the action into the environment and then you can make a choice about how you choose to act. Remember that by using reflection you are able to determine effective behaviors in your environment, and adapt in ways that will aid you in getting your needs met. If an action or reaction was ineffective, you need to plan a more effective strategy for the next time.

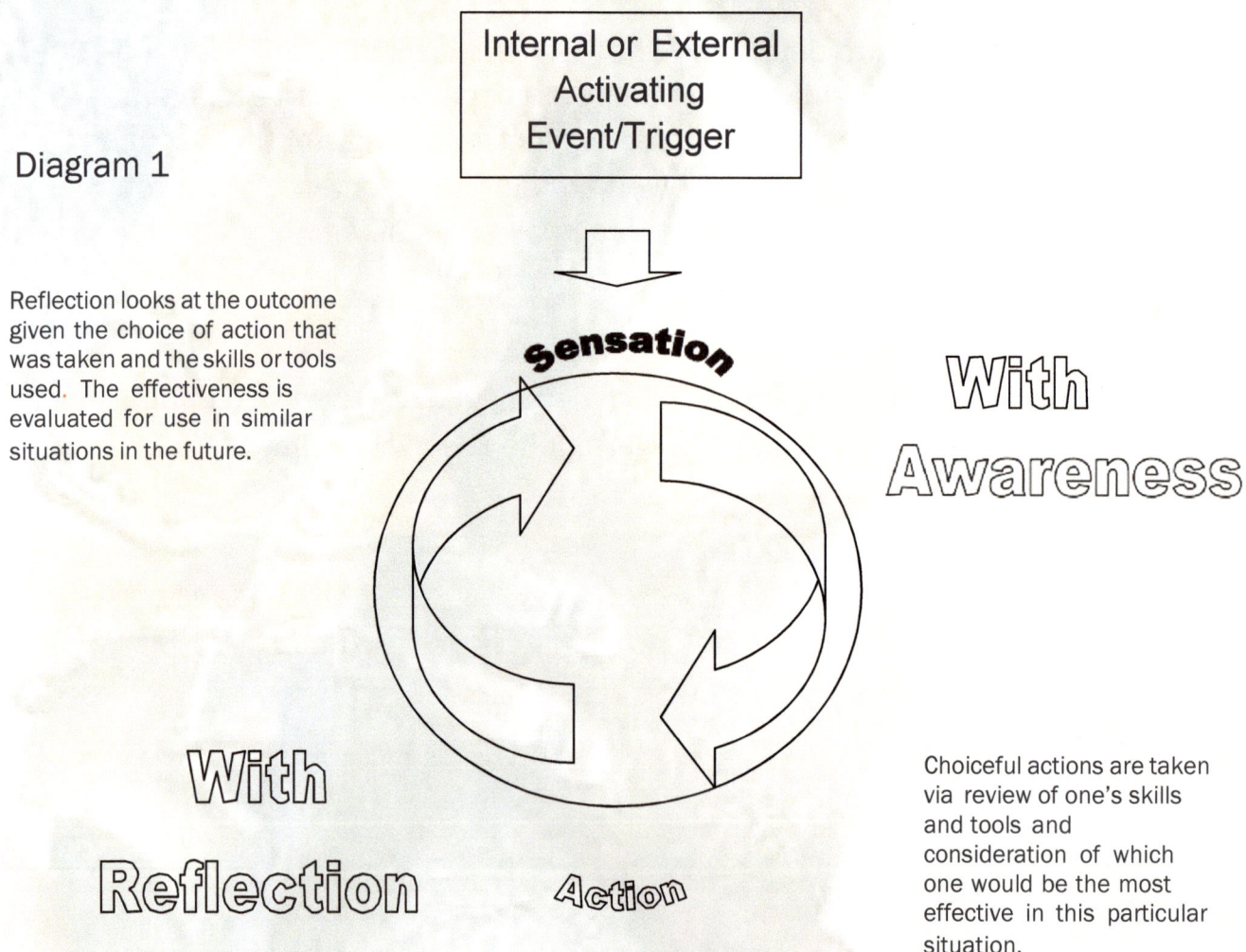

Diagram 1

Internal or External Activating Event/Trigger

Reflection looks at the outcome given the choice of action that was taken and the skills or tools used. The effectiveness is evaluated for use in similar situations in the future.

Sensation

With Awareness

With Reflection

Action

Choiceful actions are taken via review of one's skills and tools and consideration of which one would be the most effective in this particular situation.

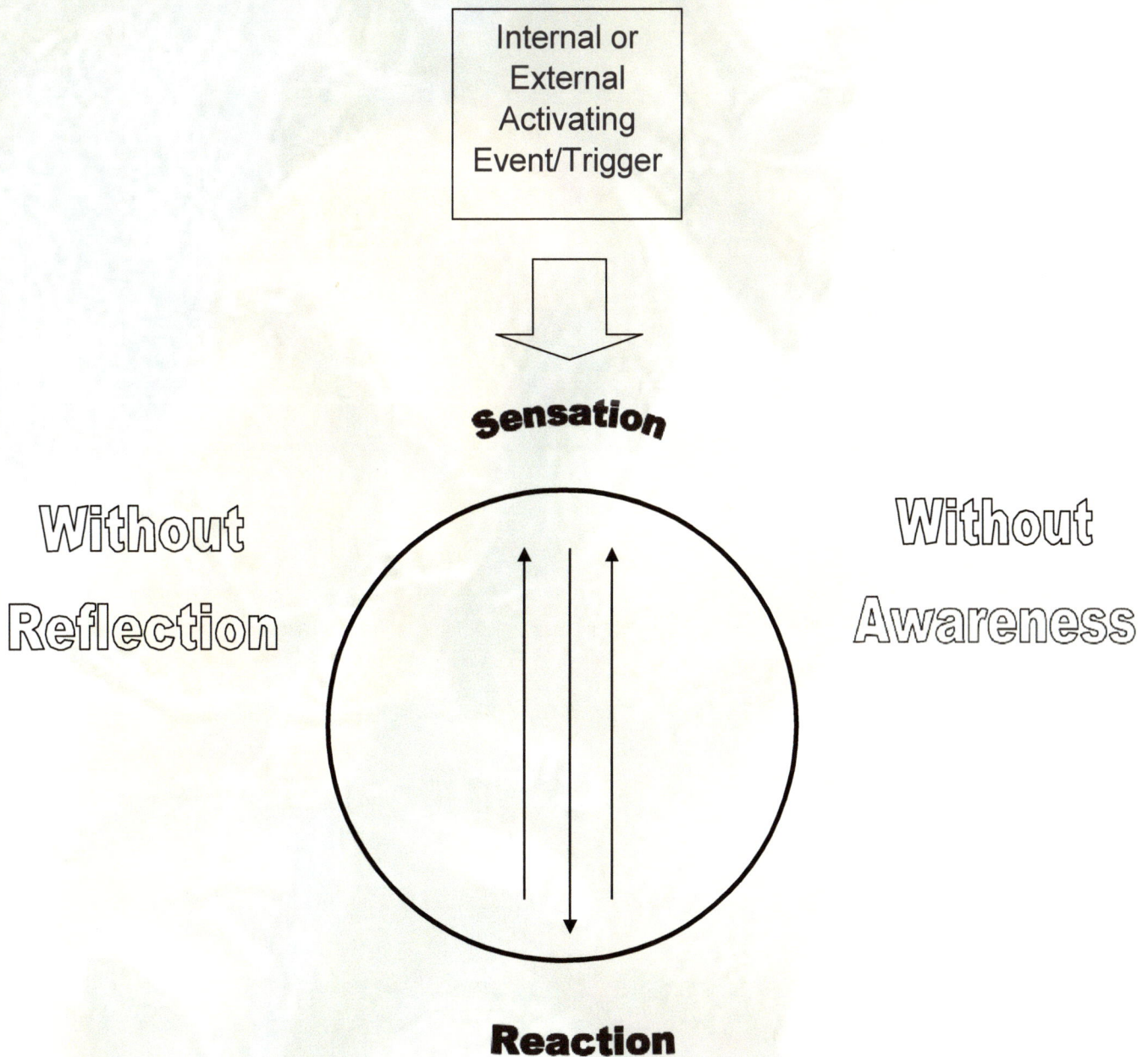

Lack of Insight

Ineffective Choice without Awareness and Reflection. Without awareness we react in our environment controlled only by our emotions. Without reflection we are apt to repeat less effective actions over and over again in our environment, become frustrated and fail to adapt in ways that will aid us in getting our needs met.

Diagram 2

```
        ┌─────────────┐
        │ Internal or │
        │  External   │
        │ Activating  │
        │Event/Trigger│
        └─────────────┘
              ⬇
```

Sensation

Without   Without

Reflection   Awareness

Reaction

The Quest Begins

"To laugh is to risk appearing a fool. To weep is to risk appearing sentimental.
To reach out to another is to risk involvement. To expose feelings is to risk exposing your true self.

To place your ideas and dreams before a crowd is to risk their loss.
To love is to risk not being loved in return. To hope is to risk pain. To try is to risk failure.
But risks must be taken, because the greatest hazard in life is to risk nothing."

William Arthur Ward

"The person who risks nothing, does nothing, has nothing, is nothing, and becomes nothing.

He may avoid suffering and sorrow, but he simply cannot learn, feel, change, grow or love.
Chained by his certitude, he is a slave; he has forfeited his freedom.

Only the person who risks is truly free."

Leo Buscaglia

Trauma / Grief Time-Line

A time line of the trauma and grief you have experienced will serve several purposes. First, it will let you examine your trauma history in a concise manner. Second, it allows you if you have a history of multiple traumas to understand the impact of those traumas on your life. Third, it allows you to determine which traumatic event is the 'hottest event'. This is important so that the worst incidents can be dealt with first and your healing begins to generalize to other less traumatic events. You may want a separate blank notebook for this exercise if you have a history of multiple losses, and traumas.

Trauma time lines can be done in a number of ways and there is not a right or wrong way to do it. Here are several methods that individuals have tried.

1. Using Table 1 make a list of traumatic events in your life along with the age(s) they occurred.

2. If you have a significant trauma history, you may want to use a notebook and use five year increments on the top of the pages.

3. You may have only a few traumatic events in your past. If so, you may just want to indicate on an arrowed time-line the age it occurred for you and what the event was at that time.

Age of first trauma ———————————————————————————— Current Age

4. Now list your SUDs for each event.

5. After listing the traumatic events in your life and labeling your current level of distress (SUDs) when you think about that event today use Table 2 to list the events starting with the one that has the highest SUDs level. So, if you have one with a SUDs of 100 start with it. If you have two that have the same number, consider which one creates the most problems for you in your daily living. Place that one first and then the other one after it. List all events that are in your danger zone numbers. If your danger zone is 100 to 30 list all items with SUD scores above 30. If your danger zone is 80 to 100 then list all your SUD scores in that range.

6. You may find a different method of doing your trauma time-line more helpful. If so, then proceed in whatever manner is effective for you.

Table 1: Trauma Time Line Event Table

Name   **Date**

Age(s)	Traumatic Event(s) Label	SUDs Level Evoked

Table 2: Trauma Hierarchy List

Age(s)	Traumatic Event(s) Label	SUDs Level Evoked

The Challenge

Choose the traumatic event that has the highest SUDs level on your list. Sit in your safe place. Allow two hours. Write out your story[1] in first person, present tense, as if it were happening now. Make sure there is a beginning, middle and end. Track your SUDs every five minutes using a copy of the worksheet on the following page. You will need one page for each day. Continue to write the story over and over again for 45 minutes. Continue to track your SUDs until they are half of the highest number, or until you have been in your safe place for two hours. Follow this procedure daily until you can write the story with minimum elevation of your SUDs. This may take three days or it may take several months. Consistency is key. Write daily. Keep in mind you will feel worse in the beginning. Usually, the first week is the worse and within three weeks usually the distress starts to drop off. However, it can take months for the intensity to start to drop, especially if your symptoms are severe. Be compassionate and patient with yourself. This is a difficult road so self-care and self-kindness is a must.

If most of the story becomes easy to write, but some parts remain difficult take the easy segments out and repeat the exercise with only the segment that remains as a "hot spot". If there are more than one of these "hot spots" repeat the exercise with each "hot spot" that remains. When you are done and none of the story remains in the danger zone level of your SUDs you are done with that event. Celebrate! I will celebrate by...

Then review your SUDs numbers on the other events on your trauma list. You will find that most of them have decreased. It is called the trickledown effect! If the next number event on your list is still in the danger zone you will repeat this exercise for it. Typically, you will only need to do one to three events to decrease all losses and traumatic events SUDs into your warning or comfort zones.

If down the road new memories emerge you can repeat this process.

---

[1] This work is adapted from the work of Edna Foa. It is based on the Cognitive Behavioral Therapy Technique Prolonged Exposure Therapy.

Tracking Sheet

Date

Interval	SUD	Interval	SUD
5 min.		65 min.	
10 min.		70 min.	
15 min.		75 min.	
20 min.		80 min.	
25 min.		85 min.	
30 min.		90 min.	
35 min.		95 min.	
40 min.		100 min.	
45 min.		105 min.	
50 min.		110 min.	
55 min.		115 min.	
60 min.		120 min.	

Notes from Today's Session

What did you notice?

Were there changes from previous sessions?

Are some areas easy to write and others harder? If so, take the hardest part to write about and repeat the process on this section until it becomes easy. Repeat with the next difficult section.

Claiming the Holy Grail

Once all the events on your time line have SUDS in or below the warning zone it is time to reap the riches of your quest. Rewrite your story as a Quest. What were the challenges that you faced?

What have you learned?

How will your life be better because you have undertaken this journey?

What are the riches you have received?

What treasures have you found?

How have you changed and grown during this journey?

How will this help you to give back to the world?

What would a great quest be without the retelling of the story? Share your new story with some people that you trust. Share it so that others might also heal. Be specific. Don't rush take your time. Create a collage! Write a blog or a book. Own your triumph!

These are the people that I trust and will tell them the story of my quest. Why will you tell them?

When will you do it?

Where will you do it?

How will you share your triumph?

Additional titles
can be found at

www.amaraquest.com